ATOMIC

Creature CAMOUFLAGE

PAUL MASON

Raintree

www.raintreepublishers.co.uk

Visit our website to find out more information about **Raintree** books.

To order:
☎ Phone 44 (0) 1865 888112
🖥 Send a fax to 44 (0) 1865 314091
💻 Visit the Raintree bookshop at **www.raintreepublishers.co.uk** to browse our catalogue and order online.

First published in Great Britain by Raintree, Halley Court, Jordan Hill, Oxford OX2 8EJ, part of Harcourt Education. Raintree is a registered trademark of Harcourt Education Ltd.

© Harcourt Education Ltd 2008
First published in paperback in 2008.
The moral right of the proprietor has been asserted.

Editorial: Melanie Waldron and Catherine Clarke
Design: Victoria Bevan and Bigtop
Illustrations: Darren Lingard
Picture Research: Hannah Taylor
Production: Julie Carter

Originated by Chroma Graphics
Printed and bound in China by Leo Paper Group

ISBN: 978 1 4062 0670 8 (hardback)
12 11 10 09 08
10 9 8 7 6 5 4 3 2 1

ISBN: 978 1 4062 0691 3 (paperback)
13 12 11 10 09
10 9 8 7 6 5 4 3 2 1

British Library
Cataloguing in Publication Data
Mason, Paul
Creature Camouflage. – (Nature's spies) (Atomic)
591.4'72
A full catalogue record for this book is available from the British Library.

Acknowledgements

The publishers would like to thank the following for permission to reproduce photographs: ardea.com (Becca Saunders) p. **19**; Corbis pp. **9** (top) (Tom Brakefield), **14** (Steffan Widstrand); FLPA pp. **6** (Larry West), **9** (bottom) (R. Dirscherl), **10** (Minden Pictures/Fred Bavendam), **12** (Minden Pictures/Tim Fitzharris), **17** (top) (Silvestris Fotoservice), **17** (bottom) (Minden Pictures/Chris Newbert), **18** (Minden Pictures/Fred Bavendam), **26** (Chris Mattison), **29** (R. Dirscherl); naturepl.com pp. **22** (Studio Times Ltd), **25** (Geoff Dore); NHPA (Jean-Louis Le Moigne) p. **21**; Photolibrary (Steve Turner) p. **13**.

Cover photograph (top) of a stick insect on a garden fence reproduced with permission of Nature Picture Library (Hanne Jens Eriksen). Cover photograph (bottom) of a leopard in a tree reproduced with permission of OSF (Digital vision).

The publishers would like to thank Nancy Harris, Diana Bentley, and Dee Reid for their assistance in the preparation of this book.

Every effort has been made to contact copyright holders of any material reproduced in this book. Any omissions will be rectified in subsequent printings if notice is given to the publishers.

Contents

Some words are printed in bold, **like this**. You can find out what they mean in the glossary. You can also look in the box at the bottom of the page where the word first appears.

HIDDEN WORLD!

The world is full of animal surprises. Shadows under a bush might hide a fierce leopard. A stick might be a deadly snake.

Stick insect

Location: *mainly tropical and sub-tropical areas*

The stick insect is shaped and coloured just like a stick.

pages 20 and 21

NORTH AMERICA

ATLANTIC OCEAN

PACIFIC OCEAN

SOUTH AMERICA

N

W E

S

Arctic hare

Location: *Arctic region*

The Arctic hare has a white coat in winter to blend in with the snow.

pages 14 and 15

Elephant hawk moth caterpillar

Location: *mainly Northern Europe*

This caterpillar camouflages itself to look like a dangerous snake.

pages 24 and 25

ARCTIC OCEAN

EUROPE

ASIA

AFRICA

PACIFIC OCEAN

INDIAN OCEAN

AUSTRALIA

Russell's viper

Location: *grassy areas in Southeast Asia and India*

This slow-moving snake has a killer bite.

pages 26 and 27

Leopard

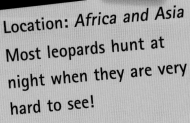

Location: *Africa and Asia*

Most leopards hunt at night when they are very hard to see!

pages 12 and 13

Wobbegong

Location: *seas around Australia*

You might not see a wobbegong until you step on it!

pages 10 and 11

This rattlesnake has excellent camouflage. It is very hard to spot!

DISGUISE IN NATURE

What is camouflage? Camouflage is a type of disguise. Camouflage makes you look like something you are not.

Camouflage can make an insect look like a leaf. Camouflage can make a fish look like a stone. A harmless caterpillar can even be camouflaged to look like a snake!

Why use camouflage?

Animals use camouflage for two main reasons:

1) They want to stay safe from **predators** – animals that are hunting them.

2) They want to be invisible to their **prey** – animals they are hunting!

disguise	making yourself look like something you are not
predator	animal that hunts other animals for food
prey	animal that is caught and eaten by another animal

TYPES OF CAMOUFLAGE

Some animals use colour as a type of camouflage. Others use shape as well.

Blending in

Many animals use colour as camouflage. It works like a soldier's uniform in the jungle. The animal's body blends in with the background.

Some animals can change their colour to fit any background. They are like soldiers changing their uniform.

Disguise

Some animals use shape and colour together as camouflage. They can make themselves look like a stick or a piece of seaweed, for example.

This tiger's stripy coat helps him blend into the grassy background.

Can you spot the poisonous fish in this photograph?

The wobbegong's camouflage helps it blend in with reefs. It also helps it blend in with sandy seabeds.

Large, dark splotches

Small, white circles

Pale yellow or greenish brown skin

Watch out!

Once wobbegongs bite, it is **rare** for them to let go!

WATCH OUT – WOBBEGONG!

Some sea animals have excellent camouflage. You have to watch out in case you tread on them!

The spotted wobbegong

The spotted wobbegong is a type of shark. The wobbegong lives in **shallow** (not very deep) water. Sometimes people step on wobbegongs by mistake! They get bitten!

FACT FILE

Camouflage: blending in

Camouflage used for: hunting

Main **prey**: crabs, octopus, fish

rare	unusual
shallow	not very deep

LURKING LEOPARDS

Dark spots surrounded by light areas are good camouflage. They look like the shapes made by sunlight shining through leaves.

Spotty hunters

Leopards have a spotty coat. During the daytime, leopards usually rest in trees. They are hidden because their coats blend with the light falling through the leaves.

Leopards usually hunt at night. Their camouflage blends with the shadows. The leopard's **prey** does not see it coming – until it is too late!

The snow leopard has a spotty white coat. It blends in with the snowy mountains.

FACT FILE

Camouflage: blending in

Camouflage used for: hunting

Main prey: antelope and deer

This leopard is difficult to see from a distance.

Did you know?

Only the Arctic hare's ears stay the same colour all year round!

The snow-white Arctic hare blends in against its snowy background.

HIDDEN HARES

Some animals change their camouflage depending on the time of year. If the landscape changes from snowy white to grassy green, they can still be camouflaged!

The Arctic hare

Arctic hares have a white coat in winter. It is hard for **predators** to spot them in the snow.

The snow melts in springtime. Most of the hares' coats change colour. They turn blue-grey. The hares blend in with their new background.

FACT FILE

Camouflage: blending in

Camouflage used for: hiding

Main predators: birds of **prey**, wolves, foxes, polar bears

THE QUICK-CHANGE NUDIBRANCH

Some animals can change their camouflage quickly. Changing their camouflage for different backgrounds makes it easier to avoid **predators**.

The nudibranch

The nudibranch is a type of sea slug. Some nudibranches eat small sea animals called **corals**. Corals join together to form underwater reefs. Reefs can be many shapes and sizes. Colours from the coral reefs get into the nudibranch's skin. The skin becomes a similar colour to the reef.

FACT FILE

Camouflage: **adaptable**

Camouflage used for: hiding

Main predators: fish, crabs

adaptable	able to change easily
corals	small animals that form underwater reefs

Predators find it hard to spot coral-coloured nudibranches crawling on coral reefs.

Some nudibranches use bright colours to warn predators that they taste bad!

Did you know?

It is male sea dragons who look after the eggs, not females.

Leafy fins like seaweed

Seaweed-coloured body

When the sea dragon stops moving, it seems to disappear!

fin   part of a fish that helps it to balance and swim

DISGUISED DRAGONS

Some animals use shape and colour as camouflage. They **disguise** themselves by trying to look like something else.

Leafy sea dragon

The leafy sea dragon lives among seaweed. It is the same shape and colour as the seaweed. It is impossible to spot!

Weedy sea dragon

The weedy sea dragon has **fins** like weeds. It is just as good at disguise as the leafy sea dragon.

This weedy sea dragon's fins look just like the weeds it swims in.

FACT FILE

Camouflage: disguise

Camouflage used for: hiding and hunting

Main **prey**: sea lice

INVISIBLE STICK INSECT

Some animals look exactly like their surroundings. These animals seem to be invisible!

The stick insect

The stick insect is one of the hardest animals to spot:

* Its body, arms, and legs are long and thin. They look like sticks.

* Its body is coloured to look like a stick.

* The stick insect lives among the branches and leaves of a tree – like sticks.

It is almost impossible to tell a stick insect from a stick!

FACT FILE

Camouflage: **disguise**

Camouflage used for: hiding

Main **predators**: birds, spiders, lizards

No wonder the stick insect is hard to spot when it is standing still!

Only male leaf insects have wings that work. Females cannot escape by flying. They rely on their camouflage to keep them safe.

Did you know?

If a leaf insect is disturbed, it starts to sway. It is imitating (copying) a leaf being blown by the wind.

LEAF INSECT

What hangs from a tree branch, and is shaped and coloured like a leaf? The answer is not always: "A leaf!" It might be a leaf insect.

Leaf insect camouflage

Leaf insects hang underneath tree branches. They look just like leaves. They can change colour to pale green or dark brown. Leaf insects can even turn patchy! This makes them hard for **predators** to find.

FACT FILE

Camouflage: **disguise**

Camouflage used for: hiding

Main predators: birds, spiders, lizards

imitate   copy

CRAFTY CATERPILLARS!

Some animals try to stay safe by disguising themselves as a fierce animal. Others try to stay safe by looking like a poisonous animal.

The elephant hawk moth caterpillar

The elephant hawk moth caterpillar has a clever disguise. It has two pretend eyes at the end of its body.

If the caterpillar is disturbed, it swells up. This makes its "eyes" bigger. The caterpillar raises its "head". It sways from side to side. The caterpillar is pretending to be a dangerous snake!

FACT FILE

Camouflage: disguise

Camouflage used for: scaring away **predators**

Main predators: birds, small **mammals** (for example, mice)

mammal   **animal that feeds its young with milk**

The caterpillar's big pretend
eyes scare away predators.

The viper's skin looks like
the pattern on army clothing.

SLITHERING SNAKE

The Russell's viper is a snake with great camouflage. In daylight, the viper often hides in grass and under bushes.

Poisonous killer

At night, the Russell's viper comes out to hunt. Its camouflage helps it blend into the shadows. It uses strong poison to kill its **prey**.

The viper hisses to warn **predators** not to attack it. Predators are scared off by the hissing noise. The Russell's viper is said to have a louder hiss than any other snake.

FACT FILE

Camouflage: blending in

Camouflage used for: hunting and hiding

Main prey: **rodents**

rodents   small animals such as mice, rats, and squirrels

THE CAMOUFLAGE KING

In this book, we have seen camouflaged animals from all over the world. Some use their camouflage for hunting. Others use it for hiding. But which animal is the king of camouflage?

The reef stonefish

The reef stonefish has the best camouflage in the fish world. It also has the deadliest poison. This is a fish to avoid when you are out paddling!

Deadly hunter

The reef stonefish lies hidden in the rocks waiting for its **prey**. Then it darts out with amazing speed. It squirts poison into its prey. The prey is soon dead!

Did you know?

The stonefish's attack is very fast. It can be seen only on slowed-down film!

Can you see the stonefish in this photo?

Glossary

adaptable able to change easily. Adaptable camouflage can change to suit lots of different backgrounds.

corals small creatures that form underwater reefs. A reef is made of the shells of coral.

disguise making yourself look like something you are not. For example, some insects are disguised to look like sticks.

fin part of a fish that helps it to balance and swim. The fin sticks out of the top of a fish's body.

imitate copy

mammal animal that feeds its young with milk

predator animal that hunts other animals for food

prey animal that is caught and eaten by another animal

rare unusual. If an animal's disguise fails only once in 100 times, for example, that is a rare event.

rodents small animals such as mice, rats, and squirrels

shallow not very deep. For example, water that comes up to your ankles is shallow.

Want to Know More?

Books

* *Amazing Nature: Clever Camouflage*, John Woodward (Heinemann Library, 2004)

* *Animal Disguises*, Belinda Weber (Kingfisher Books Ltd, 2004)

* *Nature Files: Animal Camouflage and Defence*, Anita Ganeri (Heinemann Library, 2004)

Websites

* www.childrensmuseum.org/special_ exhibits/kinetosaur/b2.html Take a look at how animals use colour to blend in!

* www.yahooligans.com Type "camouflage" into this search engine and have a look at some of the camouflage links and activities.

If you liked this Atomic book, why don't you try these...?

Index

Notes for adults

Use the following questions to guide children towards identifying features of report text:

Can you find an example of a general opening classification on page 7?

Can you find examples of non-chronological language on page 8?

Can you give examples of present tense language on page 15?

Can you find an example of detailed description of an animal on page 20?